Original title:
The Ocean's Calling

Copyright © 2025 Creative Arts Management OÜ
All rights reserved.

Author: Maxwell Donovan
ISBN HARDBACK: 978-1-80587-391-4
ISBN PAPERBACK: 978-1-80587-861-2

Where Waves Meet Solitude

I swam with fish who traded tales,
They laughed as I wore jelly shoes and scales.
A seagull stole my sandwich tray,
I shouted, "Hey! That's not okay!"

The crab taught me a dance so weird,
He twirled and flipped, while I just cheered.
The tide was high, my skill was low,
I belly-flopped; the fish said, "Whoa!"

A dolphin giggled at my plight,
"You call that swimming? Try with all your might!"
The waves played tricks, a splashy spree,
I swam in circles, feeling free.

Yet, as the sun began to set,
I realized what I might regret:
For every fall and silly splash,
I wished for more waves, not just a flash.

Harmonies of Moonlit Waters

At night, I sang to starry skies,
But fish just rolled their beady eyes.
The seaweed danced, looked quite a sight,
I joined in too, a fishy fright!

The lighthouse flashed like disco lights,
While crabs played music on moonlit nights.
A starfish joined, with arms spread wide,
"Sing louder now! Let joy be our guide!"

I tripped on waves, then slipped and spun,
The ocean's laugh echoed, oh what fun!
With bubbles rising in a bubbly beat,
The moonlight shimmered, a dance so sweet.

So, if you hear a tune at sea,
It's just the waves, and silly me.
Sing out loud, let your spirit soar,
The humor of the waters, forevermore!

Flowing through Eternity

Waves are whispering, surfboards glide,
Seagulls squawking, what a wild ride!
Flip-flops flapping, sand sticks like glue,
Sunburns and laughter, it's a grand zoo.

Paddleboards wobble, fall in with style,
Mermaids chuckle, oh what a trial!
Saltwater splashes, a slippery fate,
Tan lines and fish tales, it's never too late.

Crabs in a dance, they scuttle with flair,
Sandy-haired kiddos with seaweed for hair.
Beach balls are flying, sunscreen's on fleek,
A day by the shoreline, life's never bleak.

Ocean Echoes of Solitude

Tides are giggling, they tickle my toes,
Seashells whisper secrets, nobody knows.
Waves on a mission, all frothy and sly,
A lone fish is plotting to give it a try.

Seagulls are jokers, with snacks they compete,
Hoarding hot dogs, oh what a feat!
The horizon is laughing with clouds in a line,
While I chase my dreams on a float, feeling fine.

Seaweed confetti, a party gone wild,
Jellyfish jiving, they're just like a child.
The echoing sea sings a silly refrain,
In this watery world, joy is my gain.

Dancing with the Dolphins

Dolphins are flipping, what a grand show,
They're practicing moves for the next big pop flow.
Splashing and laughing, they nudge at my feet,
Join in the fun—oh, this can't be beat!

Fins are like dancers, swirling through waves,
Twirling and whirling, oh how it saves!
I tried to keep up, with a giddy old grin,
But I'm just a hooman, they're destined to win.

They wink and they whistle, a cheeky parade,
Under the sun, all worries do fade.
Surfing their giggles, riding the thrill,
With dolphins as partners, the fun's never still.

Timeless Tides

The clock by the beach is stuck in a loop,
Time ticks slower, join the oceanic troop.
Shells collect stories from days long ago,
But here in the present, we just laugh and flow.

Tidal waves curling, like laughter on air,
Sandcastles crumbling without a care.
Umbrellas are flying, just what could go wrong?
In this timeless bubble, we dance to a song.

With every high tide, more fun to devise,
The beach is our kingdom, the stars are our prize.
No clocks in the sand, but still, I must say,
Why count all the minutes when we can just play!

Guardians of the Shore

Seagulls squawk in silly tones,
Chasing fries and ice cream cones.
Crabs do the cha-cha on the sand,
Distracting all, it's quite unplanned.

Sunburnt knights with sunscreen swords,
Defend their towels with silly chords.
While beach balls bounce like giant fish,
Laughter swells like a well-worn wish.

Flip-flop patrols keep watch in zones,
Hoping to claim sunken ice cream cones.
Shells talk back, when you stoop down,
Whispering secrets of fishy crowns.

With sandcastles tall, we set our claim,
Ans sink our woes in this sandy game.
Guardians here, we grin and cheer,
On this shoreline, we shed all fear.

The Language of Seafoam

Waves whisper secrets as they crash,
Foamy tongues with a frothy splash.
Bubbles dance like they're on a spree,
Trying to chat with a curious bee.

Seashells giggle, all lined in a row,
Waving hello to the starfish show.
"Why don't you swim?" one clam does jest,
"I'm too busy napping," the sea turtle confessed.

Kelp sways smoothly to the sea's own beat,
Telling jokes in the current's heat.
Fish pass by in a flash and a flick,
Playing tag with a seaweed stick.

Seafoam laughs as it tickles toes,
A giggly friend that everybody knows.
In this language, we find our cheer,
With whispers of joy in the salty sphere.

Underneath Starlit Skies

Moonlight winks at the waves below,
Stars giggle softly, putting on a show.
Turtles play cards, using shells for chips,
While dolphins break dance with graceful flips.

Waves clap hands in the sweet night air,
As crickets join in without a care.
The sand shimmies under our feet,
In this quiet chaos, we find our beat.

A jellyfish juggles, quite the sight,
Glow-in-the-dark, a carnival night.
Laughter ripples through shadows so wide,
As we share dreams with the incoming tide.

Underneath stars, we find our place,
With marine comedians in endless space.
Together we laugh, together we gleam,
In this nighttime circus, we all dream.

Shores of Solitude

Here on a beach where the silence reigns,
Seagulls gossip about holiday gains.
Lonely lighthouse, standing all tall,
Wishes for friends but doesn't call.

Sand piles up in fantastic shapes,
Molding tall dwellings for silly drapes.
Waves crash gently, sharing their thoughts,
"Why so grumpy?" a clam gently prods.

A lone flip-flop has lost its mate,
Wandering off with a hopeful fate.
Starfish sunbathe, having a snooze,
Wishing for toes but left with blues.

Yet in this solitude, laughter is heard,
As seaweed dances like a bright green bird.
Shores whisper gently with warm embrace,
Even in solitude, there's room for grace.

Driftwood Dreams

On a piece of driftwood I found,
I thought I'd sail away, unbound.
But Captain Crab took charge with glee,
Leaving me stuck in a sea of debris.

I tried to surf on jellyfish,
"Ride the wave!" was my foolish wish.
But they just giggled, swam away,
Leaving me to ponder the day.

Seagulls squawked about their plans,
To grab my lunch with their beak hands.
I threw some chips into the blue,
They took them all, the crafty crew!

So here I sit with empty hands,
Adrift in thoughts of silly lands.
Where waves laugh loud and tides play tricks,
And fishes join in goofy flicks.

The Horizon's Whisper

A ship made of toast sailed from shore,
In search of a buttered galore.
But waves were munching, and they chomped,
Leaving my dreams quite soggy and plomped.

The sun wore shades, looking quite cool,
It winked at me, "You silly fool!"
While dolphins danced a comedy show,
I lost my sandwich in the flow.

Seashells laughed, playing the fool,
Calling me to the biggest cool.
But as I chased with a net and reel,
The fish just splashed, saying, "Catch the meal!"

So now I sit with sunburned feet,
Life's a laugh, can't accept defeat.
For under blue skies and salty air,
The silly moments are floating, rare.

Murmurs from the Abyss

Beneath the waves, the fish do sway,
Conducting symphonies of play.
A trumpet fish plays tunes so sweet,
While clams do tap dance with their feet.

The octopus juggles shiny shells,
As clownfish crack up with their yells.
Anemones cheer, waving their hands,
It's a comedy club in coral bands!

But then comes along a seaweed vine,
Swaying with moves that quite align.
"Join us!" they shout, "Don't be so stiff!"
I wiggled my toes with a silly riff.

Now I'm part of the underwater scene,
Flipping and flopping like a marine queen.
Who knew the depths held such surprise?
Laughter bubbles beneath these skies!

Nautical Reverie

On a ship made of paper, I sail with cheer,
With a band of fish on a grand premiere.
The captain's a trout with a shiny gold hat,
He orders smoothies, all mixed with a splat.

The sails are pillows, fluffy and bright,
But they wander away in the dim twilight.
As stars come out to peek and to sway,
The fish joke, "No naptime, not today!"

I tossed my snacks to the curious seals,
Who slid and flopped, sharing their feels.
They giggled and choreographed a dance,
Lost in the ocean's silly romance.

So here I dream under winks from the moon,
With jellyfish singing a bouncy tune.
In a world of whimsy, my heart's in control,
Sailing through laughter, I find my soul.

In Search of Coral Whispers

Bubbles burst, fish flip and dive,
A mermaid's laugh, oh how they thrive!
Crabs in tuxedos, what a sight,
Dance on the sand, beneath the light.

Octopus barista brews with flair,
Offers seaweed lattes with a stare.
Jellyfish jesters float with glee,
Who knew they'd make such fine company?

Starfish strum on coral guitars,
Singing of sailors, lost in bars.
Clams jam on pearls, a rock band's hype,
Under the waves, the stories ripe.

So if you hear a splash and a giggle,
Join the underwater dance, just wiggle.
Leave your shoes, take a fin instead,
In this sea of laughter, be well-led!

Nautical Tales of Yore

Ahoy! A tale from way back when,
A fish stole a sailor's favorite pen.
The captain chased with a mighty yell,
But the fish just laughed, saying, "Oh what the shell!"

Pirates in trunks with sunglasses on,
Searching for treasure, singing a song.
"Yo ho ho and a bottle of pop!"
Join the party, it never will stop!

A gull took the map, he was quite sly,
"I'll trade you for fries," was his sly reply.
Mermaids muttered, "Oh what a caper!"
While dolphins debated, "Who's got the paper?"

In the end, the treasure was jokes,
All laughter, no gold, just a bunch of blokes.
So grab your ship, sail the waves high,
With tales of the sea, the laughter won't die!

Driftwood Diaries

On the beach, driftwood talks aloud,
Sharing secrets with the curious crowd.
A log said, "I once swam with glee,
Until a seagull mistook me for a tree!"

Shells gossip quietly, with a wink,
About crabs who dance after they drink.
"Do you know Larry? He's rather vain,
Wears seaweed hats, thinks he's insane!"

A sea turtle chips in, "That's not the worst,
I met a fish who just liked to burst!
Pop! He went, just for a laugh,
Now he's a legend, on the ocean's graph."

So gather 'round, hear the tales unfold,
Of driftwood dreams and laughter retold.
The ocean whispers, in giggles and waves,
Join the chronicle that the sea saves!

The Infinite Blue Above

Up above, the sky's a shade of cheer,
Clouds like fish are swimming near.
A whale splashes, making the sun glint,
While a pelican winks, it's quite the hint!

"Hey look at me!" shouts a crab on a ride,
Sailing a piggyback, what a wild stride!
They laugh and frolic, they joke and sing,
Who knew the ocean was such a fling?

Seagulls compete in a flying race,
Diving and dodging, oh what a pace!
One takes a spill, falls with a splash,
Lands right on a dolphin with quite a crash!

But they just chuckle, share a grin,
In this wild sky, it's a win-win!
So lift your gaze to that bright blue hue,
And join in the fun, it's calling you!

Chasing the Sea Breeze

The wind blew strong, my hat took flight,
Chasing after it, what a sight!
I tripped on sand, then did a dance,
The beachgoers laughed, I had my chance.

Seagulls cackled, what a ruckus,
Stealing my chips? That's quite the circus!
With waves that crash and tides that tease,
I swear at times, they're such a tease!

My surfboard's ready, I'm feeling bold,
But first, let's find that ice cream cold.
With sticky fingers, I take a ride,
As the waves tumble, I screech and glide!

So here's to laughter, sand, and fun,
May this wild day never be done!
With silly moves and giggles galore,
The sea's great charm, I can't ignore!

A Symphony of Waves

The tides compose a tune so sweet,
With splashes loud and foam beneath feet.
A clam takes part, it claps its shell,
While crabs rehearse in their sandy shell.

The dolphins leap, a vibrant show,
In perfect rhythm, oh what a flow!
A conch provides the trumpet's blast,
While starfish just sway, taking it vast.

The sun takes center stage to shine,
As I conduct with a sparkling wine.
But wait, my drink is splashed away,
The waves are playful; they want to play!

With laughter ringing out from the shore,
I join the cacophony and roar!
Just music, laughter, and skies so blue,
This coastal symphony, just me and you!

Lighthouses and Lost Souls

A lighthouse stands so proud and tall,
But it can't help me, I trip and fall.
With a beacon bright, it guides my way,
Yet here I am, stuck in the spray!

The lost souls laugh, they dance around,
As I chase after waves without a sound.
They whisper jokes in the salty air,
I nod along, but don't quite care.

An octopus winks, a fishy friend,
Joining my antics, we will not bend.
In the night so dark, they light my path,
While I create my wet-footed math.

In this dance of shadows, giggles abound,
The allure of light is where I'm bound.
With mischief planned beneath the stars,
We celebrate with our sea salt bars!

Shadows Beneath the Surface

In the blue depths, what could be there?
Shadows whisper secrets, unaware.
A crab in shades, a fish with style,
They swim and groove, it's quite worthwhile.

They link and twirl, in their own parade,
While I just float, a joy unafraid.
A rock's my stage; it wobbles with glee,
It laughs out loud, "Come dance with me!"

But wait, what's that? A shadowy thing!
Careful now, it has a real sting!
Not a monster, just my lost flip-flop,
A jet ski zooms past with a big plop!

The laughter echoes, a bubbly tune,
As we splash along, beneath the moon.
With shadows prancing, a dance of delight,
We embrace the chaos, into the night!

Maelstrom of Memories

The tide pulls at my socks,
While seagulls try to steal my fries.
I laugh as waves crash rocks,
And wonder where my sandwich lies.

Beneath the sun, I start to fry,
With waterproof sunscreen, what a feat!
A crab approaches, I don't know why,
I think he's judging my beachy seat.

Flip-flops snap like rubber bands,
Chasing kids who bump their heads.
Sand gets everywhere, oh the strands,
As I trip over beach umbrellas' spreads.

I build a castle, oh so grand,
But the waves have quite the plans.
It crumbles fast, just like my sand,
At least I've perfected my beachy dance.

Reflections on the Water's Surface

Mirrors of the sea, oh how they gleam,
But dive in, and they shatter your team.
I splashed my friend, what a silly scheme,
Now she's plotting revenge, or so it would seem.

The fish are laughing, or so I swear,
Their little fins dance; it's not quite fair.
I chase them round with quite the flair,
But all I net is seaweed hair.

A gull swoops down, it's filled with sass,
Stealing my lunch, that little brat.
I flip it the bird—it's high-class grass—
Now all that's left is a sad old hat.

The sunset paints a crafty show,
While I struggle with my floaty foe.
I sink, I float, then slip and go,
Next time I'll stick to sunsets; they glow.

Nightfall at the Harbor

The harbor lights twinkle, oh so bright,
As ships dance away in the fading light.
A catfish grins, to my delight,
With a wink, it whispers, 'Fear not the night.'

Chandeliers of stars appear overhead,
While I snack on popcorn, no fear or dread.
But wait, that's not popcorn! I might be misled—
Just fishy snacks, I once again thread.

Boat horns blare like a loud old tune,
Everyone's singing beneath the moon.
A seal pops up, it knows how to croon,
As I do the cha-cha and trip on a spoon.

The fishermen chuckle, so full of cheer,
While I'm tangled in nets, let's make that clear.
But give me a laugh with a pint of beer,
For this night-ready harbor brings me near.

Castaways in Midnight's Embrace

Stranded at sea with nothing but beans,
Lost in thoughts of unfortunate scenes.
A shipwrecked sandwich, what could it mean?
A buffet of seagulls and silly routines.

We build a raft of driftwood and dreams,
But the tide takes it all, or so it seems.
I shout, 'Send us snacks!' through laughter and screams,
As the fishes roll their eyes in our schemes.

With makeshift hats of seaweed and fun,
We crown ourselves kings till the morning sun.
It's a royal mess, but we still run,
Sipping saltwater, oh what have we done?

In this midnight embrace, we find our glee,
As laughter echoes across the sea.
We'll toast to our dreams, just you and me,
Not quite marooned, just silly and free.

Serenity in the Abyss

In the deep where the fish wear suits,
They attend a ball with dancing boots.
The crabs play cards, the clams all cheer,
Underwater fun, no need for fear.

A jellyfish floats by in a hat,
Sipping on seaweed like a fancy cat.
The starfish are judges, they take their seat,
While seahorses race, oh what a feat!

Shrimp spin tales of grand sea quests,
While the octopus plays all sorts of pests.
With bubbles of laughter, they frolic and play,
In this watery world, life's a cabaret.

So come take a dip, don't just observe,
In the humor of marine life, you won't swerve.
Dive in today, let your worries cease,
In this abyss, find your joy and peace.

Boundless Blue Skies

Sky so vast, like a canvas free,
With clouds that giggle, come dance with me.
Seagulls gossip about the tide's new prank,
While dolphins take selfies, oh how they'll crank!

Flip-flops forgotten, we run on the beach,
Burying our troubles just out of reach.
Sandcastles rise, then come crashing down,
A royal decree from the tide, our frown!

Kites that twirl with grand crazy flair,
They spool their strings in the salty air.
Laughter erupts as the waves crash loud,
We form a parade, both silly and proud.

Under boundless skies, let's all just play,
Take a ride on a wave, let worries stray.
The sun's warm embrace, a shimmer divine,
In this funny world, we'll all intertwine.

The Heart of the Gale

Whirlwinds of laughter spin in the air,
As sailors wear socks that they'll never pair.
The ships are all swaying, a waltz on the sea,
With pirates who giggle like children at tea.

Every gust brings a song in disguise,
Seagulls audition, their talent's a surprise.
They squawk out a jingle, the catch of the day,
While fish flash their scales in a dazzling display.

Down below, mermaids giggle and twirl,
Swapping their shells for a shiny pearl.
A crab runs a mile in his tiny best shoes,
In this heart of the gale, there are laughs to peruse.

So if you hear thunder, don't run in fear,
It's just Mother Nature trying to cheer.
Join in the fun, let the waves spin you 'round,
In this crazy squall, pure joy can be found.

Reflections of a Deep Sea Dreamer

At the depths where the sun seldom shines,
A fish named Frank writes his grand designs.
With a pencil made of coral, he scribbles away,
Dreaming of bubbles that float and sway.

He tosses his thoughts to the ocean floor,
Where sea turtles read and the sand dollars score.
The seaweed's his audience, they rustle in glee,
While octopuses sketch in the deep blue sea.

Every wave that rolls brings a fresh new idea,
A jellyfish juggles, and crowds all cheer.
With the echo of laughter, the currents align,
As Frank spins his tales, oh-so divine.

So dip down below for a whimsical ride,
Where each wave whispers secrets so wide.
In these deep reflections, where dreams swim and swirl,
Join Frank in his fantasy, let laughter unfurl.

A Journey Through the Mists.

A crab with a hat and a wig,
Sings loudly to a playful pig.
The fog rolls in with a cheeky grin,
While fish do a dance, oh what a gig!

Seagulls are squawking a tune so bright,
Arguing over the snacks in sight.
One stole a sandwich, oh what a sneak,
While others just squawk, 'That's not polite!'

A whale made some blubbering jokes,
Telling tales of all silly folks.
The starfish laughs with a wink and twist,
While dolphins dive in, calling like stoked folks!

So wade in the waters, make a splash,
Chasing jellyfish in a wild dash.
Surfer seals ride waves, full of cheer,
Just watch out for the seaweed stash!

Whispers of the Tides

An octopus working a night shift,
Can tie your shoes with a funny twist.
While shoreside, a clam in its shell,
Claims to have tales that are hard to resist.

Salty snacks leave crabs in a fright,
When seagulls swoop down in full flight.
The tides make whispers, oh what a sound,
As beach balls bounce in the moonlight.

A fish in a bow tie does the jig,
Bouncing around with a dance so big.
The jellyfish laugh with their glow so bright,
While letting the sea bubbles do the big swig.

With splashes and giggles, we dive and play,
Building tall castles that wash away.
In this funny world where the sea greets,
We'll dance with the waves till the end of the day!

Echoes in the Abyss

In the depths where the shadows tease,
A shrimp plays games and tries to please.
It twirls and spins, a bright little spark,
While eels giggle in their seaweed leaves.

A pirate fish tells of buried gold,
But it's just a hoax, or so we're told.
Caught in a net with some algae knots,
The humor's so rich, it's far from old!

The squid's in disguise, what a funny sight,
Making faces deep in the night.
With ink clouds swirling, a grand parade,
Where sea creatures join, what a delight!

In the deep where the barnacles sing,
They laugh and reflect on the joys of spring.
With echoes of laughter, the sea resounds,
As the absurd antics happily cling!

Beneath the Seafoam Sky

Bubbles are rising with giggles so deep,
Under the sea, all secrets we keep.
Starfish in boots strut around with flair,
While the seaweed's dancing, a lover's leap!

A clownfish jokes with a serious sting,
"Why so blue? Just let the fun swing!"
The currents ripple with laughter and cheer,
As dolphins leap high and birds take wing.

A hermit crab found a house so neat,
But lost his way on his tiny feet.
With crabs as his guides in a wobbly chase,
They giggle and wiggle, a comical feat!

So splash in the sun's warm golden light,
With seafoam toppings, this life feels right.
In the surf and the sand, with laughter and glee,
We'll dance till the stars claim the night!

Sirens of the Deep

Down by the shore, the seagulls squawk,
Mermaids giggle as they take a walk.
Their hair's a mess, all tangled with seaweed,
But they sing with joy, that's all they need.

A crab in a tux, ready for a dance,
Tries to impress with a sideways glance.
He wears a top hat, but trips on the sand,
A funny little sight, no one had planned.

Fish in tuxedos swim past with flair,
While octopuses juggle, it's quite the affair.
A dolphin brings snacks, a party on waves,
With splashes and laughter, oh how it saves.

The tide rolls in, the sun's sinking down,
Whispers and giggles are heard all around.
With laughter so loud, the ocean's alive,
In this wacky world, sea creatures thrive.

Currents of Desire

A fish in a bow tie is making a scene,
Chasing a shrimp, all dressed up like a queen.
They swim in circles, it's quite the chase,
While turtles just laugh, they slow down the pace.

A whale with a hat tries to sing a tune,
But ends up spitting water, oh what a boon!
Nearby a seal slides down a slippery rock,
Rolling in laughter, they're quite the flock.

The jellyfish dance in a wobbly line,
With swirls of color, they think they look fine.
But one does a flip and gets stuck in a net,
All in good fun, their laughter's a bet.

With bubbles and giggles, the currents all sway,
As the crabs do the cha-cha and pufferfish play.
In this splashy world where desires are bright,
The ocean's a party, everything feels right.

Lullabies from the Lighthouse

A lighthouse keeper sang to the moon,
With a voice so funny, it caused quite a tune.
The gulls joined in with their squawking delight,
As waves rocked the boats in the shimmering night.

Children on the shore built castles with glee,
Forgetting their snacks—now there's sand in the brie!
They chase the tide with their tiny, wet feet,
As the waves laugh back, their rhythm so sweet.

A crab on a bicycle rides down the pier,
With a bucket of popcorn, he's ready to cheer.
He tosses the treats to the seals down below,
In this lullaby world, they put on a show.

The lighthouse shines bright, a beacon of fun,
As starfish join in, singing one by one.
With a wink and a splash, the night carries on,
In this sleepy sweet place, where no one feels dawn.

Saltwater Serenade

At dawn, the seashells gossip and squeak,
Sharing wild secrets, as they chat and peek.
Anemones giggle, their colors ablaze,
While starfish are plotting a grand stage to craze.

Dolphins flip tricks, splashing the air,
Crabs clap their claws, with salty flair.
A fish with a mustache tells jokes on the rise,
As everyone chuckles with smiley surprise.

Seagulls swoop low, they're stealing the show,
Swiping some fries from a tourist below.
With a dance and a dip, they put on a feast,
In this salty amusement, there's fun for the least.

The sun sets slowly, drapes gold on the waves,
While laughter and joy are the treasures one saves.
In this playful lagoon, so wild and so free,
The serenade of saltwater makes them all agree.

The Soul of the Sea

Bubbles rise and fish do dance,
Seagulls squawk, it's their chance!
A crab in shorts, so quite the sight,
Sandy toes, what a delight.

Jellyfish float with silly grace,
Waves come crashing, oh what a race!
Mermaids giggle, hiding their tails,
While starfish tell the best of tales.

A whale who thinks he's quite a star,
Sings along to the beachside bar.
With every splash, a joke's revealed,
In salty air, laughter's sealed.

Shells and seaweed join the fun,
Cracking jokes 'til the setting sun.
The sea is a party, full of cheers,
Join in the laughter, forget your fears.

Kelp Forest Whispers

In the kelp where fish play hide and seek,
A sea cucumber tells tales so unique.
With tentacles waving, an octopus grins,
As sea otters roll in their furry spins.

Crabs wear hats, they look so fine,
Laughing while doing the conga line.
Eels are gossiping with sleek charm,
Making currents twist and twirl, oh so warm.

An urchin jokes with a spiny sneer,
"Life's more fun when you're without fear!"
Meanwhile, the anemones dance with glee,
In this underwater jamboree.

Kelp sways gently, like a funky beat,
As fish all gather for a disco meet.
With bubbles popping like confetti rain,
It's underwater joy, no room for pain.

Glistening Reflections on the Tide

The sun dips low, it's time to rest,
Crabs in sunglasses just look their best.
A dolphin spins, showing off his flair,
While beach balls bounce without a care.

Seashells are gathered for a grand parade,
With hermit crabs marching, all charades!
They giggle as waves roll in and out,
Creating a scene that's full of clout.

A sandcastle king wears a crown made of foam,
While shells serenade him — it's their home!
With a wave of the tide, they all stand proud,
Having fun, laughing, feeling the crowd.

The glow of sunset, a sparkly show,
Kites flying high as the warm winds blow.
The sea reflects fun in every way,
Join the festivity; it's a beachy stay!

Songs of Faraway Shores

From sandy beaches, the tunes arise,
With shells as drums, they play their prize.
A pelican croons a silly song,
As gulls join in, all singing along.

Turtles groove with their slow-motion moves,
In the rhythm of waves, each one proves.
The clownfish jest, throwing seaweed confetti,
Bubbles of laughter, nobody's petty.

Every splash tells a story or two,
Of treasure maps, and the ocean's view.
With pirate patches and wooden legs,
The sea is playful, no need for dregs.

As night takes over, stars start to gleam,
Mermaids line up for the closing theme.
With joyous voices, they'll sing till dawn,
In harmony with waves, as the night goes on.

Waves Whisper Secrets

Waves crash with giggles, you see,
Telling jokes in a splashy spree.
Seaweed dances, quite the sight,
Shells chuckle softly, day and night.

Seagulls squawk a silly tune,
As crabs waddle, quite immune.
Starfish play cards on the sand,
While dolphins flip, oh isn't it grand?

Fish pass notes in bubbles bright,
A gossip club under moonlight.
An octopus dons a silly hat,
Joining the laughter, imagine that!

In this watery world we find,
A comedy show, one of a kind.
So grab your towel, come join the cheer,
The sea's sense of humor is truly clear!

Depths Unveiled

Beneath the waves, where light is dim,
Fish wear glasses, what a whim!
Crabs with bow ties walking tall,
Make a splash at the underwater ball.

Anemones play hide and seek,
While turtles race, oh so sleek.
The eels tell tales of daring dives,
With laughter that keeps the ocean alive.

A sardine school forms a parade,
While a clownfish jokes, never afraid.
Sea cucumbers might join the fun,
Sunken ships shine like a prize won!

Mysteries lurk, yet spirits soar,
In this deep blue, laughter galore.
So take a dip, come swim along,
In these depths, there's always a song!

Sirens Sing at Dusk

As the sun sets, mermaids giggle,
While fish join in, with a splash and a wiggle.
Their chorus of laughter fills the air,
Making sailors stop and stare.

With scales that shimmer, they twist and swirl,
Leading boats on a wild whirl.
"Try our singing, it's quite a hit!"
They serenade, while they laugh and spit.

The laughter echoes over the sea,
As bubbles float, so wild and free.
A crab sings baritone, what a sound!
While octopuses play the seaweed round.

At dusk, the waves dance with glee,
Who knew the deep was so funny?
So pull up a rock, enjoy the fun,
While sirens bask in the setting sun!

Tides of Memory

Waves wash in with a story to tell,
Of beach ball battles and ice cream fell.
Flip-flops giggle on sandy shores,
As laughter echoes through open doors.

Seashells lined up like a comedy act,
Each with a punchline, a well-timed fact.
A beach umbrella winks at the sun,
While seagulls squawk, "Is this all in fun?"

Kids build castles with moats, not walls,
Each wave a chance for a tumble and fall.
Kites dance above with laughter untold,
In these tides of memory, their stories unfold.

So gather the tales, let joy be your guide,
As the ocean whispers, with laughter beside.
In every ripple, a chuckle you'll find,
The spirit of fun, adventure entwined!

Heartbeats in the Sand

I built a castle, oh so grand,
But then it crumbled, like my plans.
A crab marched in, my knight so bold,
I swore it stole my treasure of gold.

The waves laughed hard, a jolly tune,
As I chased after bubbles, driftwood, and moon.
My bucket's full of seashells bright,
But empty of fish that dart and bite.

Seagulls swoop, they steal my fries,
They seem to think that I'm their prize.
I wave my hands, they just will squawk,
While I hop sideways, trying to walk.

With footprints dancing upon the shore,
I splash around, can't help but roar.
For in this place, where the tides do sing,
I just might forget that I can't swim!

Coral Rainbows and Twilight

Coral reefs wear vibrant attire,
Fish parade like a swimming choir.
I brought my snorkel, looking so sleek,
But swallowed a wave, now I can't speak.

The sunset paints the water so bright,
I try to pose, but lose my sight.
The waves keep crashing, and I fall flat,
A beachside dance with a clumsy splat.

Turtle floats by with a wink and grin,
Taking his time, I can't keep in.
He rolls his eyes as I flail and dive,
A pool of laughter, barely survive.

Oh, to be free like the pirate's glee,
Chasing my dreams in a jellyfish spree.
But alas, the tide pulls me away,
While I thrash about like a beach ballet!

Beyond the Seagrass

In waters deep, I took the plunge,
But ended up with a finned grunge.
I waved to dolphins, thought I'd fit,
They just laughed, like I was it.

Seagrass tickles my toes with glee,
I swear I heard a fish call me "Flea."
With goggles fogged, I lost my way,
Just a beach bum who's gone astray.

An octopus winked, said, "Try my dance!"
But with his eight arms, I missed my chance.
We spun in circles, what a sight,
Then he waved bye, so long, goodnight!

Later that day, on soft warm sand,
I built a new castle, fine and bland.
Who knew that being a fishy friend,
Would end in laughter, but never blend?

Tidal Whispers

Waves whisper secrets, oh so sly,
I wish I could understand their why.
With every splash, a joke they tell,
I laugh along, hoping all is well.

My beach ball flew, a bird took flight,
I chased it down with all my might.
The sand kicked up, I did a flip,
The lifeguard grinned, "That was a trip!"

Seagulls clatter, they steal my snack,
Screaming like they're under attack.
I swing my arms, trying to defy,
But they're cunning and fast, oh my, oh my!

As sun sets low, the glow we find,
In this goofy show, oh never blind.
For every wave comes with a laugh,
Making memories, my seaside staff!

Ocean's Embrace

Splashing water on my toes,
Seagulls dive like flying foes.
I wave my arms, try to swim,
But end up with a silly grin.

Sand sticks to my sunscreened nose,
I trip on waves like clumsy crows.
Shells sing songs of joy and cheer,
But all I hear is my own leer.

Kisses from the Sea Breeze

A gentle puff, a cheeky tease,
It ruffles hair with such great ease.
I laugh as my hat takes a flight,
Chasing seagulls, oh what a sight!

Jellyfish dance, oh such a fright,
I jump and squeal, it's quite a sight!
The waves hum tunes of salty glee,
"Catch me if you can!" they decree.

Messages in the Bottled Blue

I found a bottle, thought it grand,
Filled with seashells and a soft strand.
I opened it with hopes so high,
But only found a fishy fry.

With scribbled notes and doodly art,
The world seems silly, and so is my heart.
Each bottle near the shore I see,
Might just hold another fishy spree!

Secrets carried by the Winds

Whispers from the waves so sly,
They share the jokes the crabs comply.
"Why did the fish blush?" they jest,
"Because it saw the ocean's best!"

A breeze brings laughter, wild and loud,
As kites and kids run, all so proud.
I ask the winds for tales to bring,
Yet they just giggle, oh what a fling!

Dreams Adrift on the Horizon

A boat made of pasta, it floats in the sea,
With a captain named Larry, who talks to a pea.
They sail through the laughter, the waves full of cheer,
Chasing jellyfish jelly, while sipping cold beer.

The fish all wear bowties, they dance in a line,
While seagulls play banjos, oh isn't it fine?
They sing silly songs, with a splash and a twirl,
As the ocean flips pancakes, just like a wide whirl.

A turtle in sneakers races past with a grin,
While crabs in tight pants decide it's a win!
With flippers for feet, and a hat on his shell,
The world under water is simply a spell.

So come join the crew, leave your worries on shore,
Where the sea's full of giggles, and laughter galore.
With dreams made of bubbles, we'll float on this ride,
On a ship of pure nonsense, with joy as our guide.

Waves of Longing

The waves sing a tune that tickles your toes,
They whisper of secrets in languages prose.
But seagulls can't help it, they squawk out of tune,
With a chorus of echoes from morning to moon.

A crab in pink crocs struts along with some flair,
While dolphins in tuxedos flip high in the air.
With surfboards made of waffles, they ride on the foam,
Leaving syrupy trails in this oceanic home.

The starfish hold parties, with lights made of shells,
They giggle with clams, telling tall fishy tales.
So, pack up your worries, and bring lots of snacks,
For the waves are alive in their zany hijacks.

Caught in waves of laughter, let joy take the lead,
The beach is a playground, where fun takes the heed.
Each splash holds a secret, each ripple a smile,
In this zesty mishmash that goes on for a while.

Beneath the Celestial Waves

Beneath azure ripples, the party's begun,
With mermaids in shades, under stars they have fun.
Octopuses juggling, with flair and with art,
While fish wear sunglasses, they play from the start.

With treasure chests full of candy and glee,
They trade all their trinkets for jellyfish tea.
The sandcastles giggle, they bounce like a ball,
While sea snails in helmets compete in a crawl.

Sharks dressed in tuxes serve snacks on the side,
While squids play charades, and the waves gently glide.
It's a whimsical world, where laughter runs free,
With bubbles of joy that float wild in the sea.

So, dive in the madness, make waves that won't end,
In this funny blue realm, where giggles descend.
Every splash tells a story, every ripple a laugh,
As we dance with the currents, oh what a good gaff!

Embrace of the Blue

In a sea full of winks, and laughs that are bright,
The fish share their gossip under pale moonlight.
With crabs in a polka-dot, cha-cha parade,
And sea cucumbers pulling pranks that they've made.

A whale with a bowtie leads tap-dancing crabs,
While seahorses giggle, they form little jabs.
As waves shake their feathers, the sun starts to cling,
To this merry brigade in a splashy zing fling.

The dolphins are mischief-makers, it's true,
They ride on the ripples, and plan a hullabaloo.
With a flip and a twist, they defy all the rules,
While the walrus, in laughter, juggles bright jewels.

So dip into laughter, let joy overflow,
For the sea's full of mischief, you'll never outgrow.
With every sweet splash, feel the giggles set free,
In the embrace of the blue, come with laughter, just be!

Underwater Waltz

Fish in top hats dance a jig,
They spin and twirl, oh what a gig!
Crabs do the cha-cha, clams keep time,
All join in for an underwater rhyme.

Seahorses grace with fancy flair,
Dolphins giggle, no need to care.
Jellyfish glide in a wobbly line,
Shells clap to the beat of the brine.

Mermaids laugh, their hair in a mess,
Twisting and turning, what a success!
A conga of fish, both big and small,
Under the waves, they're having a ball!

Bubbles rise high, popping with cheer,
Every flip and flop brings more near.
The ocean floor becomes a stage,
For a silly show, they all engage.

Solitude in the Siren's Song

A lonely fish hums a tune so sweet,
Waves bump n' grind, what a treat!
With every note, the currents sway,
Even the sea garbage starts to play.

A flounder frowns, "I want a duet!"
But all the octopi just fret.
Crabs are setting up a crabby band,
"Now who can hold a seashell hand?"

Turtles wish they'd learn to rap,
But they're too slow for this musical map.
The starfish jive with their five-point flair,
Too slick to care, they dance without a care.

Shells start clapping, seaweed sways,
All join in these funny displays.
Under the surface, the fun can't stop,
Till a big wave sends them all to flop!

Chasing the Rising Tide

A seagull squawks, "Catch me if you can!"
While clams and scallops form a plan.
They all line up in a wobbly queue,
As the tide rolls in, they're feeling anew.

A crab makes a dash, his shell a bright red,
While snails can't keep up, they drop their bread.
"Oysters don't run!" the clam does boast,
But he'll be the last in this tidal toast.

Dolphins leap high, in a game of tag,
While sea urchins just wave and brag.
The tide comes in and out it goes,
While laughter spills from fins to toes.

"Faster!" yells a fish with a sparkling tail,
But the turtles just chuckle and set the sail.
Oh, what a chase, oh, what a ride,
In this watery world where fun won't hide!

Beneath the Marine Veil

A sea cucumber wobbles along,
Singing a very off-key song.
"Dancing is hard when you're soft and round,"
He sighs while bopping out loud, unbound.

Coral reefs giggle, colorful and bright,
As fish in tuxedos swim into sight.
With a flip and a flop, they dodge every swirl,
Creating a spectacle in a watery whirl.

The sea anemone shakes its funny head,
"Why not join the party instead?"
But a shy goldfish whispers, "Not today,
I'll just observe the silly display!"

In this playful realm beneath the foam,
Where laughs and giggles create a home.
Under this marine veil of delight,
Life's a funny ride, and oh what a sight!

Embracing the Horizon's Edge

I set my sail with a heavy snack,
A sandwich tucked snug in my pack.
The seagulls laugh as they swoop and dive,
My lunch now flies, oh what a survive!

With sunscreen smeared from head to toe,
I dance on the beach, just watch me go!
I kick up sand like it's confetti,
While dodging a wave that feels too petty.

I think I saw a whale wave back,
But it was just a big old stack.
Of seaweed flapping in the breeze,
Reminding me to aim for the seas!

The waves roll in, a funny cheer,
I chase them down; they disappear!
Oh, salty air, your jokes are grand,
As I trip and tumble in the sand.

Journey through Aquatic Realms

With goggles on, I dive so deep,
Searching for treasures, secrets to keep.
Instead, I find an old lost shoe,
Who knew the sea has one-footed crew?

A crab waves me with its tiny claw,
I swear it's judging; it's got some saw!
I try to dance with fishy friends,
But they just swim off; my fun ends.

Oh look, a dolphin doing a flip,
I join in, take my own wild trip.
But I belly flop, what a grand sight,
Even the fish burst out with delight!

At sunset, I sit with a soda in hand,
The waves whisper jokes, oh it's grand!
As night falls, I giggle at the tide,
Every splash feels like a joyful ride!

Celestial Navigations

The stars above twinkle with glee,
I chart my course, like Captain Me!
A rubber duck floats, my fleet so bright,
Navigating troubles, a comical sight.

The moon winks down at my silly crew,
A fish in a cap? Oh, is it true?
We sail on waves made of jelly and cream,
Star-gazing feels like a floaty dream!

My compass spins, I'm lost, oh dear!
But I laugh it off, got nothing to fear.
An octopus offers directions with style,
Its ink map seems to mislead all the while!

Underneath it all, I sing a tune,
With crabby back-up 'neath the silver moon.
While drifting along with my goofy friends,
Life on the water, where fun never ends!

Voices from the Cresting Waves

The waves giggle as they crash and play,
Making silly sounds, come what may.
I stand on the shore with my big ol' hat,
Wishing the beach would just be less flat!

A fish pops up, with a cheeky glare,
"Bet you can't splash!" it dares me to dare.
I leap and I flop, oh what a mess,
The ocean laughs at my splashing finesse!

A conch shell whispers secrets so sweet,
Telling tales that are hard to believe.
As the tide ebbs back, I've made a new friend,
A sea cucumber! Who knew it could bend?

In the surf, I wave at passing boats,
With stories to share, oh how it gloats!
Funny voices fill the sunny shores,
With laughter that echoes forevermore!

Beneath the Starry Waters

Bubbles rise like tiny dreams,
I dive in search of fishy schemes.
Seaweed dances, a wavy beast,
I think it's time for a beach ball feast!

Jellyfish float with grace and flair,
I wave to crabs without a care.
I chase a dolphin, thinks I'm fast,
But I trip on sand, I fall at last!

Starfish giggle on rocky beds,
With arms like sponges, wiggling heads.
There's laughter echoing all around,
Beneath the waves, joy can be found!

So grab your goggles, jump right in,
Join this splashy, silly spin.
With fins and flippers, let's all play,
In underwater land, we'll laugh the day!

Whims of the Wind

The wind whispers secrets to the sea,
Telling jokes about a fish named Lee.
He swam too fast, got stuck in a net,
   But laughed it off without a fret!

Seagulls squawk, they're quite the jest,
Trying to steal a child's sandcastle quest.
They swoop down low, with their beak so sly,
While kids just laugh and watch them fly!

A crab in sunglasses struts along,
Dancing to a mermaid's favorite song.
He twirls and spins with such great flair,
   While beachgoers stop and stare.

Let the wind tickle your cheeks and hair,
With these playful moments, we've plenty to share.
So come on down for laughter and fun,
Where the whims of the wind never come undone!

Shimmering Blue Fantasy

In a sea of sparkles, I see a fish,
Wearing a crown, making quite the wish.
He swims in circles, with glee and delight,
Hoping for snacks, with a wink and a bite!

Octopuses juggling, oh what a sight!
They toss sea shells, oh such funny fright!
A clam sings loudly, off-key and bold,
As the dolphins giggle because it's so old!

A whale with a hat, oh what a fun view,
He wears it best, in shades of blue.
We'll have a party, with barnacles dancing,
In our shimmering world, all goofily prancing!

So dive right in, let's make a splash,
Join this wild party, there's no time to dash.
In this fantasy deep, we'll laugh and explore,
With every wave crashing, we'll always want more!

Horizon's Farewell

As the sun dips low, the sky turns gold,
The silly sea gulls dance, oh so bold.
They squawk and swoop, with twisty spins,
While waves clap hands like zany twins!

Sandy toes and laughter fill the air,
A crab wearing shorts gives everyone a scare.
He scuttles quick, playing hide and seek,
But slips on a wave, oh what a cheek!

The horizon blushes, a fiery show,
As kids build castles, with cups in tow.
A beach ball flies and bounces around,
With every happy yell, joy is found.

As the day ends, we raise our glass,
To funny moments that forever last.
With salty winds and giggles that swell,
We wave to the sunset, and bid it farewell!

Journey to the Shore's Edge

I packed my bags with snacky treats,
A towel, sunscreen, and big bare feet.
The sand's warm hug and waves that play,
Screaming 'come hither'! Let's surf today!

A seagull swoops, then steals my lunch,
I chase it down, but oh, what a bunch!
With crumbs in my hair and laughter loud,
Who knew the shore would feel so proud?

I chased a crab; he waved me off,
With a pinch on the toe, I let out a scoff.
A flip-flop flies, my sandals have fun,
Twirling and flipping, it's a beach bum run!

The sun dips low, the sky turns gold,
I'll trade a seashell for stories untold.
In this sandy chaos, a new friend I find,
Waving goodnight to the beach, so kind.

Dancers of the Waters

The waves are wiggling, they find their groove,
In aqua ballet, they shimmy and move.
Splashes of laughter, a fresh salty spray,
They trip on some driftwood, but hey, that's okay!

A seal takes the stage in a seaweed crown,
With a backflop, a belly flop, joy never frowns!
Dolphins are diving, oh what a sight,
Dancing through bubbles, oh, what pure delight!

The jellyfish sway, that's one funky crew,
Wobbling and wobbling in all shades of blue.
I join in the fun, a twirl and a spin,
Who knew aquatic dance could spark such a win?

At the end of the show, I throw up my hands,
In applause for the waters and their funny plans.
With sand on my toes, I munch on some fries,
In this swirling circus, it's a beachside surprise!

Secrets in the Coral Garden

Underwater, buddy, there's a party tonight,
Where fish wear bow ties, and clams hold tight.
Corals in colors that paint the sea floor,
With secrets galore and so much in store!

A starfish winks, oh what a surprise!
While sea urchins giggle with gleeful eyes.
I peek through the kelp – what's this? Oh, my,
A crab in a top hat just passing by!

Seahorses gossip about the latest trends,
In their underwater gowns, they say "no offense!"
I join in the chatter, despite the strange stares,
Who knew the deep would have parties to share?

As night falls gentle, the lanternfish gleam,
Waving my goodbyes, I float in a dream.
The garden's a wonder, filled with delight,
Tomorrow's secrets await in the light!

The Call of the Sirens

Oh, the sound of laughter drifts over the tide,
With voices like honey, they giggle and glide.
Sirens of fun, oh what a commotion,
Inviting the sailors with easy devotion!

One tosses a seashell, it lands with a plop,
While I chase it down, I trip, flip and flop.
Their laughter bursts out like bubbles in foam,
"Stay for the party, just leave the dry dome!"

I pull on my swimsuit, the water looks grand,
But a wave gives me wedgies, oh isn't it planned?
Sirens just cackle, their game is so sly,
With flips and with splashes, I'm such a wet guy!

As I limbo beneath seaweed, I can't help but cheer,
For sirens of mischief who spread so much cheer.
With good humor flowing, and tired legs too,
I dance with the tides, and say, "Let's continue!"

Crashing Waves and Hushed Cries

Waves are dancing, what a sight,
Except that I forgot my kite.
Seagulls squabble, squawking loud,
While I just trip, it's quite a crowd.

Buckets spill and laughter roars,
As children seek out sandy shores.
A crab scuttles, runs like mad,
I scream, forgetting I'm not sad.

Sandcastles rise, then swiftly fall,
I build one bigger — oh, so tall!
But the tide's a sneaky beast,
My masterpiece? Just a rare feast.

The sun goes down, the fun won't end,
For seaweed's play is on the mend.
With all the chaos, I might cry,
But instead, I laugh and wave goodbye!

Sands of Time Beneath the Sky

Footprints left then washed away,
How did I lose my shoe today?
The sand holds secrets, oh so deep,
But all I find's a nap, not sleep.

A beach ball flies, then hits my head,
Laughter echoes, oh dread indeed!
My friends will never let it go,
Each poke and tease, a new show.

Shells are scattered, treasures small,
I wonder if they heard my call.
In chasing dreams, I'll lose the sun,
Then blame the tide for all the fun!

As the gales whisper with a cheer,
I shout, "Next year! I'll bring my gear!"
But until then, I'll dance and sway,
With sandy toes, I'll bumble away!

Constellations of the Sea

Stars above and fish below,
Who knew sea stars steal the show?
Mapping tides like constellations,
While I ponder fishy sensations.

A dolphin jumps, oh, what a tease,
The splash hits me, oh, the freeze!
Soaked to skin, I shake and laugh,
Sailing away on a water craft.

Jellyfish glide, their sting's a fright,
But all I see is a glow at night.
I wave hello, but they just grin,
Is this where my journey begins?

In the salty air, life's a play,
Who knew I'd make friends in this way?
With giggles and splashes, it feels so free,
Under this sky, I swim with glee!

Anemones and Moonlight

Anemones sway in twilight's gleam,
Whispers of water, what a dream!
I accidentally trip on a rock,
And blame it on waves as they mock.

Moonlight dances, twinkling bright,
But my focus is on avoiding bites.
Pesky fish nipping at my toes,
I laugh, it's more fun than it shows.

A wave crashes, and I lose my hat,
My friends now laugh like it's a spat.
An octopus grins with seven charms,
While I shout, "Hey! Get off my arms!"

Yet under the stars, I spin around,
With salty joy, I'm ever bound.
For in this dance with liquid light,
Funny moments keep the spirit bright!

Horizon's Embrace

Seagulls squawk, they steal my fries,
As waves crash loud, they're in disguise.
I wave back, they laugh and sway,
Quite the show in this salty play.

I tried to swim, but forgot my snacks,
A fish swam by, it gave me flack.
"You think you own this sandy beach?"
I slowed to chat, but then it screeched.

A crab danced by in fancy shoes,
With a pinch that warned me of bad views.
I tripped and fell, rolled in the sand,
The sun smiled down, "You're quite the brand!"

So let's toast to the waves and fun,
With ocean antics, never done.
Grab your shades and let's dive in,
This goofy life is where we win!

Nautical Dreams

Sailing high on a rubber duck,
The captain's hat made me quite struck.
The crew are squirrels, they steal my hat,
Oh, what a journey, look at that!

The waves, they laugh, as I start to slip,
Oar in my hand, I start to trip.
"Don't rock the boat!" the ducks all squeal,
But my dance moves are the real deal!

I spotted a mermaid, I waved quite bold,
She threw back her head and laughed, so bold.
"Bring me a snack; it's been a slow day!"
"Here's a sandwich!" I shouted, "Hey hey!"

As we sail off into sunset bright,
With squirrels dancing, what a sight!
In nautical dreams, fun's never far,
Just keep your snacks, and you'll raise the bar!

Reflections in Saltwater

I looked in the tide, who's that I see?
A goofy grin staring back at me.
A seaweed toupee was quite the catch,
My look so fresh, it's hard to match!

With jellyfish umbrellas, we dance all day,
While crabs in tuxedos proudly sway.
The sun takes a dip in the glistening sea,
As beach balls argue: "Who's funnier, me?"

I found a message in a bottle, oh dear,
"Bring chips to the party!" it read loud and clear.
So I took off running, feet in the sand,
Toward beach-lovin' critters; oh, it was grand!

With laughter and waves, we make quite the scene,
Fun's our elixir, oh so serene.
So stick with me here, on this sun-kissed spree,
Reflections in saltwater, just you and me!

The Call of the Abyss

In the deep, where things get weird,
A creature said, "Come on, you're smeared!"
With fangs, it grinned, "Join the brine,
We've got games that are quite divine!"

A fish ran by, in neon hues,
"Try my dance; you'll win some shoes!"
I stumbled and fell, but caught the beat,
Legs of a jelly, I danced in defeat.

Octopi offered a grand buffet,
"Eat all you want; shrimp it your way!"
But I looked down, felt my tummy churn,
"Really, my friends, it's salt I'll spurn!"

So I waved goodbye to the undersea trend,
With giggles and gurgles, I'll recommend.
In the call of the deep, let's keep it light,
With laughter and fun, it feels just right!

Heartstrings at Sea's Edge

Seagulls squawk like they're in a band,
Dancing on the shore, can you understand?
My flip-flop flew off, it's chasing a fish,
I'll need a new pair, it's my childhood wish.

The tide rolled in with a sneaky grin,
Oh wait, there goes my sandwich—can't let it win!
Crabs do the cha-cha, they think they're so sly,
I laughed so hard, I forgot how to dry.

The jellyfish waved, it looked quite absurd,
I tried to pet it—oh, how I disturbed!
With every splash, my shoes filled with brine,
I'm now a mermaid—you know, just divine!

Sandcastles topple, oh what a disgrace,
Where's my kingdom? All gone without trace.
But with every wave, I can't help but cheer,
Life's a beach party, come join the fun here!

Memories Beneath Moonlit Waves

The full moon smiles, what a silvery sight,
I tripped on a shell, oh what a night!
The stars are winking, with mischief so bold,
As I dance with the seaweed, if only I'm told.

Dolphins can laugh, they flip with such grace,
But watch out for fish; they'll put you in place!
A crab pinched my toe, what a funny surprise,
It said I looked tasty, what a bag of lies!

Mermaids are gossiping, sharing their lore,
"Did you see her hair? It washed up on the shore!"
I joined their tea party, forgot the real world,
With sandy cupcakes and seaweed unfurled.

But as night fades, the tide starts to run,
I gather my memories, every single one.
With laughter and joy, I bid them farewell,
Till the next glorious night, I'll remember it well!

Coastal Echoes

The coast is alive with whispers of fun,
Shells tell our secrets, one by one.
My hat flew away, oh what a sight,
It danced with the gulls, took off in flight!

The sea foam giggles, tickling our toes,
"Careful!" it warns, as it bubbles and goes.
I swear I heard laughter from fish in the deep,
Oh, the mischief they promised, I couldn't keep.

A clam tried to sing, but sang out of tune,
I joined the chorus, under the moon!
With each wave that rolled, my worries would fade,
Best friends with the ocean, I've got it made!

The beach ball escaped and drifted away,
I chased it with joy, oh what a display!
All creatures are giggling, as tides ebb and flow,
Together we frolic, let the good times grow!

Cradle of the Currents

The currents rock gently, what a wild ride,
I surf on my float, with laughter inside.
A seagull swoops down, steals my last fry,
I wave him a bye, with a wink of my eye!

The sun has a glare, oh what a fantastic show,
It painted the sky in a glorious glow.
I'm building a fortress, but it's slowly washed down,
The tide just said, "Sorry, you're losing this crown!"

Merfolk do cartwheels, they cheer and they splash,
While I hide my snacks in a very swift dash.
The waves clap their hands, a bubbly applause,
As I tripped on a net; nature gives me its flaws.

With dolphins as pals, and laughter galore,
I wouldn't trade this for gold or for more.
So here by the swells, let's shout and let's cheer,
Life's a grand adventure, let's dry off and sear!

Beneath the Celestial Blue

Beneath the waves, a fish does dance,
He's doing the tango, giving us a glance.
With seaweed hair and snazzy shoes,
He sways to the rhythm of watery blues.

A crab plays drums on a coral throne,
While jellyfish groove in a moonlit zone.
They've got the moves, oh what a sight,
These undersea parties go on every night.

A whale sings high, it's a comic tune,
While dolphins jump, under the moon.
They giggle and splash, it's quite the play,
Who knew the sea had such a cabaret?

So next time you frown, just remember this,
The ocean's full of laughter and bliss.
With creatures that twirl and sing with glee,
Under the waves, life's one big spree!

Currents of Longing

The beach chair's nice, oh what a nest,
But my drink's gone warm, I need a rest.
I called to the waves, 'Bring me a brew!'
But they just laughed, as if they knew.

A seagull swoops down, thinks it's a thief,
Snatches my sandwich, that pesky chief!
With a squawk and a flap, it took to the sky,
Now I'm left hungry, and I wonder why.

My sunscreen's gone rogue, it's slippery slick,
I smeared it on my face, what a funny trick.
Now the sand's my friend, sticking with pride,
I'm a walking beach ball – oh, what a ride!

So here I am, lost in sea fun,
With gulls and sand, I guess I've won.
As the waves swirl in a playful race,
I laugh at the ocean's quirky embrace!

Echoes of the Deep

In the deep blue, I whisper my plea,
To find lost treasure — or maybe a key.
But all I find are fish who stare,
They bubble back laughter, without a care.

A clam tried to tell me a secret or two,
But all it did was giggle and spew.
The tale it spun was all out of whack,
Ending with, 'Hey! Where's my snack?'

Even a shark came to join the jest,
He chuckled and swam, 'I'm simply the best!'
With a toothy grin, he winked at me,
And said, 'Just don't be my next entrée!'

So I leave with a grin and a watery cheer,
The ocean's full of humor, that much is clear.
With each gurgled laugh from the creatures so deep,
I find joy in the tides, as the giggles creep!

Sand Between My Toes

With toes in the sand, I took off my shoes,
But now they are buried, oh what a snooze!
A kid nearby digs a giant hole,
I fear I might end up as part of his goal.

The sun's blazing down, it's turning me red,
While seagulls circle, I wish they'd be fed.
They squawk and they dance; I mock their routine,
Oh to be free like a bird, how serene!

Then comes a wave, full of jokes and splashes,
It finds my towel, oh how it crashes!
Now I'm soaked and laughing, I take it in stride,
The sea's just a prankster, but I'll abide.

So here I will stay, with sand on my feet,
Counting the giggles, I find life's sweet.
With oceanic humor, I'm happy to coast,
In the laughter-filled waves, I'm the ultimate host!

www.ingramcontent.com/pod-product-compliance
Lightning Source LLC
Chambersburg PA
CBHW060134230426
43661CB00003B/415